DATE DUE
REMINDER

JUL 2 ~ 20~2

SEP 1 1 2002

7/24

AUG 3 0 2011

DEC 1 8 2012

Please do not remove

this date due slip.

A Clam Named Sam
by
Lee DeVitt

Illustrations
by
Chris Millis

A Clam Named Sam
by
Lee DeVitt

Illustrated
by
Chris Millis

Published by
Lone Oak Press
1412 Bush Street
Red Wing, Minnesota 55066
info@loneoak.org
ISBN 1-883477-56-5
Library of Congress Control Number: 2001097486

Printed in Canada

A Clam Named Sam
by
Lee Devitt

Illustrated by
Chris Millis

Lee DeVitt

This tale of whimsy woven with truths
was written years ago for my then granbabies
Nancy Ann and Barbara Lee

I dedicate it to them and
to all curious chldren everywhere.

And I give grateful thanks to
the following special people:
Patty Blakesley, my daughter, for her loving support.
Gay Nelson, West Tisbury Children's Librarian
for her fine, insightful suggestions.
Karen Achille, friend, for her publishing
know-how and enthusiasm.
Ray Howe, for his most helpful expertise.

Enter

Sam is a happy clam. Who has ever heard of a happy clam?
Not many of you, I'll bet. 'Cuz most clams don't talk.

You know the expression, "Clam up?" For that matter, who ever
heard of a clam with a name?

Sam's mother had always wanted a name,
so she named her first
baby Samuel.

Sam was happy to have a name.
In his little clam voice
he would sing,
"I'm Sam the Clam."

It made Sam happy to sing. If you are ever on Martha's Vineyard,
a big island six miles off the part of Massachusetts, Cape Cod,
that hooks out into the Atlantic Ocean on a map of the United States,
you will have to listen for a clam singing. That is where Sam lives.

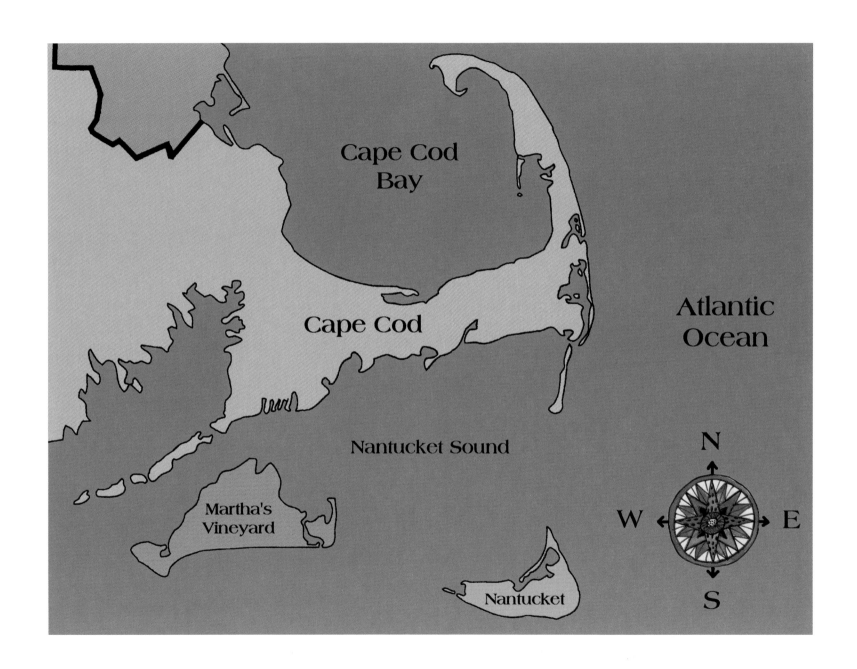

Cape Cod
Bay

Cape Cod

Atlantic
Ocean

Nantucket Sound

Martha's
Vineyard

Nantucket

N

W   E

S

Well, actually, he lives in the sandy and silty bottoms of bays and ponds. Of course, you and I would have to listen very carefully to hear him.

Sam did not always agree with his mother, especially when she warned him not to sing so loudly as the clam diggers would be more likely to find him or to stay away from certain places that were becoming polluted and dirty.

One day Sam was lazily enjoying
the warm water
in a small pool left
as the tide went out.

Suddenly he was being lifted high in the air.
Then, just as suddenly, he was dropping down
and d-o-w-n-n-n.

He landed with a big thud!

Luckily for Sam, the gull that dropped him to break his shell had missed the roadway and Sam landed in a clump of marsh grass.

Some children had seen the gull
carrying the clam and pointed to it, at the same time
yelling for their parent's attention.

That was Sam's lucky break!
The gull did not return to try again.

Very slowly Sam recovered enough
to dig through the mud and sand to the
nearby pond and into the bottom.

He stayed there for a long time before
he was over the shock - closed tight as a clam.

In a few days he felt better and was busy
filtering food out of the water — happy
as a clam can be and singing,
"I'm Sam the Clam. A lucky clam I am."

Do you know why Sam sang?

Well, he had known too many clams so uptight
with their shells closed together most of the time.

They did not grow very fast and were so sad.

Sam decided when he was very young
that he would never be sad.

He decided to be happy no matter what!

He often felt lucky and happy not to end up
in a clam digger's pail to be carried home for supper...

Someone else's supper that is!

When Sam was young he had a scary tussle
with a starfish. Luckily the starfish was also young
and not nearly as strong as his daddy was.

The starfish wrapped his arms tightly around Sam
and tried to pull and pry his shells apart.

He tried and tried
But he could not.

Not even the least, little bit.

Sam used all his muscles to hold together tightly.
You know how sometimes kids struggle and tussle
and neither wins so then they give up and walk away?

Well, that is what Sam and the starfish did.

But Sam was not dumb! He knew a larger, stronger starfish
would have taken him out of his protective shells. That would
have been the end of Sam! So he has been alert for starfish
ever since and moves away as fast as he can.

Isn't Sam something else when you
know how happy he is?

He sings,
"I'm a lucky clam.
I'm a happy clam.
I'm Sam the Clam, I am, I am."

Do you want to know more about Sam?

Have you ever wondered about your Grandma and Grandpa?
Maybe you are lucky enough to know and see them.

Have you ever wondered about their grandparents?

Your Great, Great Grandparents?

Sam had a Great, Great Grandpa, too.
As clams go, he is quite famous.

Part of his shell is in the State Museum
for people to look at.

Why? Well, I will tell you.

Long ago, Indians used clamshells as money.
The Indians who lived along the coast used pieces
of old clamshells washed up on the beach.

If there were layers of purple in the shell
it was called Black Wampum and worth twice
as much as White Wampum.

Sam's Great, Great Grandpa had been very, very purple.
He was used in trading, buying and selling for a long, long time.

Now you may find a piece of wampum
if you go beachcombing.

That is what it is called when people walk
up and down the beach looking for things
the wind and the waves wash up on the shore.

So, as you look among the different shells and stones,
you may get lucky and find some Wampum.

Of course, it would be more fun to hear Sam singing.

You'll have to be ever so quiet,
and listen very carefully to hear
above the noise of the water.

"I'm Sam the Lucky, Happy, Clam.

Sam the Clam am I!"

About the Author

Living on Martha's Vineyard - an island off the south coast of Massachusetts - Lee DeVitt fondly recalls her childhood in the Washington, D.C. area and her summers in Nebraska with relatives.

She spent many years in the midwest attending High School in Elmhurst, Illinois, college at Carleton in Northfield, Minnesota where she graduated Phi Beta Kappa with a Natural History major and then teaching high school biology in Janesville, Wisconsin.

A Mother of three , she has always loved beachcombing since living on the very beach edge near Tillamook. Oregon and the Whitstable-Tankerton area of Kent, England.

She is a strong conservationist and enjoys the many aspects of the wonderful natural world.

"Carry in carry out!"

Empty cans, bottles, plastic bags or can-rings, even balloons, that are left on or wash up on the beach can be a danger for fish, turtles and other animals that live in the sea and birds as well.

Ask your parents to be sure their garbage and sewage is not adding to the pollution problem.

Have fun looking and listening for Sam. Let me know if you hear him singing.